Survival Skills

Tony Norman

INSIDE STORY

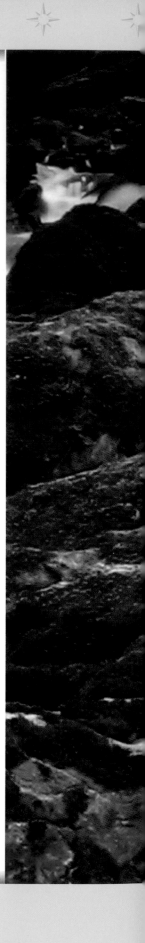

Copyright © ticktock Entertainment Ltd 2006
First published in Great Britain in 2006 by ticktock Media Ltd,
Unit 2, Orchard Business Centre, North Farm Road,
Tunbridge Wells, Kent TN2 3XF

ISBN 978 1 86007 847 7
Printed in China
9 8 7 6 5 4 3 2

The author would like to thank Patrick McGlinchey, from
the Backwoods Survival School in Scotland.
The publishers would like to thank Natural Pathways
Survival Company for their help in making this book

Picture credits (t=top; b=bottom):
13T Tim McGuire/CORBIS; 15B, 17B Mike Forti; 17T Hannah
Nicholls, Natural Pathways Survival Company; 20B Free Nature
Pictures; 24-25 Dynamic Graphics Group/IT Stock Free/Alamy

Every effort has been made to trace the copyright holders, and we
apologise in advance for any unintentional omissions. We would be
pleased to insert the appropriate acknowledgements in any subsequent
edition of this publication.

Contents

On the Edge

Most people live in the comfort zone. They see the same streets, houses and faces every day. It's good to break free, once in a while. A hiking trip through hills and forests can be exciting, but hikers need to be properly prepared.

GOING HIKING

Even something as simple as going for a walk in the country can be risky for people who don't have the knowledge to prepare properly. Hikers must know what to do if weather conditions are more severe than expected, if there are injuries, or if the group becomes lost.

SURVIVAL KNOWHOW

Every year, hikers become lost and have to spend the night outdoors. This book explains what they should do in this situation and why. Survival skills save lives – and not just for hikers. Knowing what to do is essential for anyone who spends time in the wilderness. It may even save the lives of passengers stranded in a remote area after an aeroplane crash.

A hike is a long walk in the countryside. Hikers enjoy the lovely scenery, fresh air and exercise.

SURVIVAL FACTS - DID YOU KNOW?

Swiss army knives have many useful features including a saw, blades, a tin opener, a hook and scissors. The latest also give readings for altitude (height) and air temperature.

FIRE

WATER

FOOD

SIGNALLING

A mirror can catch the sun and show rescuers the way to go.

Properly prepared, surviving in the wilderness is a thrilling experience.

Day Hiking

It is best to go hiking with somebody else or in a group. Hikers should always tell someone where they are going and what time they plan to return. Then, if help is needed, the rescue team know where to start their search.

PREPARING FOR THE HIKE

Hikers don't need a lot of equipment for a day's walk. The only items they are likely to need are a map, a compass, water and food. Sun cream is also needed in sunny weather. Good boots and the right clothes will help keep the hikers comfortable.

PREPARING FOR SURVIVAL

Although they are unlikely to need it, hikers must also take a survival kit with them. A pocket knife can help build a shelter. A lighter or matches will light a campfire. Whistles, mirrors, or even a bright bandanna, can all be used to signal for help. Other items that may be useful are a bivvy bag, strong thread, safety pins, and a torch. A first aid kit is a must, and hikers should also know the basics of first aid.

Nobody thinks that they will become lost. Hikers should always carry a small survival kit with them.

Climbing high mountains is difficult and dangerous. Survival skills are essential.

SURVIVAL FACTS - DID YOU KNOW?

Rescuers need to know your name, your medical condition and who to contact in an emergency. Carry a tag with this information on it. You may be in a coma before you are found.

This first aid kit has dressings, tape, bandages and antiseptic wipes.

TRUE STORIES

1972. A plane crash in the Amazon jungle killed 91 people. A German teenager was the only one to survive. She walked alone for 11 days and was saved by local hunters.

COMPACT FIRST AID

Chocolate is a good high energy snack - but it will melt if the day is too warm.

Sun cream protects against sun burn. Use it on any sunny day, even in winter.

Navigation

Hikers must have a good map of the area they plan to explore. Even then, it is easy to get lost. The sun can help. It rises in the east and sets in the west. If hikers walk towards the setting sun, they know they are headed west.

THE RIGHT EQUIPMENT

Hikers should always carry a compass and a map, and know how to use them. Check the map frequently to make sure the group is on the correct path.

DON'T PANIC

People who get lost in the wild must stay cool and calm. Groups should never split up to look for help. Staying together, close to the original route, improves the chances of an early rescue.

NEVER AT NIGHT

Trying to walk to safety at night is a very bad idea. It is very easy to slip or fall in the dark, even with the aid of a torch. Being lost can be scary, but being badly hurt is far worse.

If you become lost look for features that you can find on a map: streams, tracks, huts, fences etc.

A compass, used with a map, will help hikers find the correct path.

SURVIVAL FACTS - DID YOU KNOW?

Young kids are told to hug a tree if they get lost in the woods. It's a simple way of staying safely in one place until they are found. It's harder for rescuers to find somebody who moves.

Keep a detailed map of the area in a transparent waterproof bag.

TRUE STORIES

Montana, 1823. Hunter Hugh Glass was attacked by a bear. He was left badly hurt and alone. Hugh crawled 160km (100 miles) to get help. It took him six months.

To find north, turn the compass until the red needle lines up with the N.

A GPS (Global Positioning System) will pinpoint where you are and can show you where to go.

What To Wear

It's hard to know what to wear in the wilds. In mountain areas, the weather can change in a flash. It is best to wear layers of clothes. Add or take away layers to avoid getting too hot or cold. If it gets colder, sweaty clothes can cause hypothermia.

Breathable fabrics are waterproof, but allow sweat to evaporate from the body.

WALKING BOOTS

Boots should be waterproof and cover the ankles to help prevent sprains. They should have a good tread on the sole to grip the ground.

HATS

Hats hold in body heat in cold weather and give shade and cover when it's sunny. Hats help to prevent heatstroke, which causes dizziness, headaches, stomach cramps and vomiting.

BANDANNA

A large square of brightly coloured cloth has many uses. In the cold a bandanna can be used as a scarf, in the sun it can prevent sunburn. In dusty conditions it can be tied over the face for protection.

Walking boots will protect feet on rocks or forest trails.

SURVIVAL FACTS - DID YOU KNOW?

Never wear a new pair of boots on a hiking trip. That is a sure way of getting blisters, which will turn a dream trip into a nightmare!

The jacket you choose will depend on the conditions you expect to hike in.

TRUE STORIES

1992. Colby Coombs was climbing in Alaska when an avalanche hit. Two of Colby's friends died and he was badly hurt. Colby fought the snow for four days and made it out alive.

Lightweight, waterproof jacket.
Weight: 275 g

Warm, breathable waterproof jacket.
Weight: 725g

Fleece jacket with high neck for added warmth.
Weight: 445g

Food and Drink

Most trekkers eat and drink more than they usually do when they are out in the wild. Climbing hills or walking forest trails burns a lot of energy. The advice is "eat before you are hungry, drink before you are thirsty."

DRINK PLENTY

Most people need 2-4 litres of water a day, more if they are doing something active like hiking. Hikers should make sure they carry enough water with them.

A hot meal is a real boost. It might be worth carrying a lightweight stove with you.

TOP TREK FOODS

High energy foods are perfect for a trek into the wild. Try bread, rolls, pita bread, oatmeal biscuits, crackers, boiled eggs, fresh fruit, dried fruit, nuts and cheese. Tins of baked beans, fruit, chicken and tuna are good too, but remember to take a tin opener. Carry snacks to eat between meals. Hikers must carry all the food they need for their trip. There are no shops out in the wilderness.

In hot weather it is particularly important to drink regularly to prevent dehydration.

Trail mix is made from nuts, seeds and dried fruit.

SURVIVAL FACTS - DID YOU KNOW?

Kisses under the mistletoe are part of Christmas. But don't let that cosy image fool you. Mistletoe is dangerous. The berries are poisonous and must never be eaten.

TRUE STORIES

Utah 2003. A boulder fell on Aron Ralston as went through a wild canyon. Aron had to cut off his arm with a penknife to break free. Then he walked to safety.

Energy bars usually contain fruit and whole grains.

These bars are strips of dried fruit, a convenient way to carry a healthy high-energy snack.

In An Emergency

It is very important to make the right plans and take the right equipment on a wilderness trip. Being prepared helps prevent an emergency situation from turning into a disaster.

The right clothes and enough food will help to prevent hypothermia.

ASSESSING THE SITUATION

You are lost in the middle of a wilderness. What do you do? The first thing is to assess your situation. Does anybody know you are missing? How long will it be before somebody comes looking for you? This will give you an idea of how long you might have to survive. The next thing to consider is warmth. It's usually a good idea to build a shelter, and in extreme conditions, it is essential.

THE NEXT STEP

If you are not going to be rescued for several days, you need to find a source of water. Most water needs to be purified before it is used. In desert conditions, collecting water may be more important than building a shelter. Finding food is unlikely to ever be a top priority, as humans can survive several weeks without eating.

Build a shelter in daylight, before the rain. Then it's there when you need it.

SURVIVAL FACTS - DID YOU KNOW?

There is a saying to show survival priorities: you can live three minutes without air, three hours without shelter, three days without water and three weeks without food.

A simple shelter is to tie string between two trees and cover with a tarpaulin.

TRUE STORIES

Washington 1995. A pilot crashed in a mountain area. He was not badly hurt, but died of exposure. His survival kit, which might have saved his life, was found in his car back at the airport.

For a debris shelter, lean a pole against a tree and stack branches along the side.

Cover the frame with smaller branches and leaves.

Shelter

Building a shelter is a top survival skill. In forests, this can be done by leaning a line of branches against a pole fixed between two trees. This is called a 'lean-to' and has sloping sides like a tent.

IN THE BAG

Big plastic bags can be worn like a sleeping bag, keeping body warmth in and rain out. Bright colours are best. They can be seen by rescuers. Cut a hole in the bag for your head.

SNOW CAVES

People lost in the snow can find shelter by digging a snow cave. A cave one metre deep and two metres long is perfect for one person. Any bigger and the cave is difficult to keep warm. There must be an air hole in the roof and the way in should be lower than rest of the cave. Snow caves are warmer than the icy air outside.

Sleeping on the ground is cold. Line the shelter with blankets, small branches or grass.

Don't make your shelter too big. A small shelter is easier to keep warm.

SURVIVAL FACTS - DID YOU KNOW?

Frostbite is the freezing of the skin, often on the hands, feet, ears, nose and face. Danger signs are when the skin turns a grey-yellow or grey-blue colour.

To build a dugout, find a dry dip in the ground. Hollow it out further.

TRUE STORIES

The Rockies, 1993. A boulder fell on
Bill Jeracki's leg. Bill had no shelter and
knew he could die. He cut off his leg with
a pocket knife to break free.

Cover with a
tarpaulin or
small branches,
leaving a gap to
get in and out..

Use leaves
and dirt
to cover
the shelter.

Campfire

A campfire gives warmth, a way to boil water to make it safe to drink, heat for cooking and a means to dry wet clothes. It also keeps wild animals at bay and acts as a signal to show rescuers where you are.

A large fire provides warmth and comfort, but requires a lot of wood.

BUILDING A FIRE

Always carry matches, a lighter or a flint. Before starting the fire, collect all the wood you will need. Pile up dry twigs, leaves and pine needles and light the fire. Once the tinder is burning, add small pieces of dry wood. As the flames grow, bigger pieces of wood are added. Campfires should always be built before night falls.

SAFETY FIRST

Campfires can start a bush or forest fire. The safest place for a fire is on a patch of clear ground, away from trees and bushes. Never build a fire on rocks near a river, or take stones from a river bed. The wet rocks can explode when they heat up.

A ring of stones around the fire will help stop it from getting out of control.

SURVIVAL FACTS - DID YOU KNOW?

If the ground is very wet or covered with snow, build the fire on a base of green logs. Lay several logs next to each other, then add another layer at right angles.

Waterproof matches are an easy way to start a campfire.

TRUE STORIES

1994. Italian Mauro Prosperi got lost in the Sahara desert for nine days while taking part in a marathon race. He had to eat bats to stay alive!

A modern flint and steel produces a shower of very hot sparks.

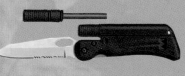

A lighter produces a steady flame. Choose a windproof lighter.

Drinking in the Wild

Drinking enough water is good for your mind as well as your body, and you need a clear mind to survive in the wild. It is not safe to drink water straight from rivers, lakes or streams. Water must be boiled for several minutes to kill germs.

Water always flows downhill Look for streams in valleys.

LIFE OR DEATH

Humans can live up to three or four weeks without food. Without water, humans die in just a few days. Every drop is vital. Well prepared hikers will have iodine tablets which kill germs and make dirty water pure. Cloudy water must turn clear before it is safe to drink.

SOURCES OF WATER

Rainwater is usually safe to drink without treating. Rain can be collected in pots, tins, jars or plastic sheets. Water can also be squeezed out of moss or cactus plants.

Cacti are not a good source of water. Many plants are poisonous to people.

SURVIVAL FACTS – DID YOU KNOW?

Never eat snow – melt it first. If you don't have anything else, melt snow in your mouth. But it's usually more efficient to break through the ice of a stream to get water.

In sunlight, plants 'sweat' water which can be gathered and drunk.

TRUE STORIES

Vietnam 2004. Bui Duc Phuc, a fisherman was lost at sea in his small boat for 14 days. He survived by drinking his own urine and eating a raw sea turtle.

Tie a clear plastic bag over a leafy part of the plant and seal it tight.

Water will condense on the bag. Use many bags to collect enough water.

Finding Food

Most people will never need to find their own food, but it is good to know what to do in a real life-or-death situation. Catching mammals is hard, and it is usually better to hunt insects or frogs. Never eat plants unless you are absolutely sure they are safe.

FISHING

A fishing line and a few hooks are easy to carry and they can save lives when trekkers get lost. Trapping fish is also a good idea. Use bait to lure the fish into a net. Fresh fish is easy to cook over a campfire and it tastes good too. If the fish has a slimy skin, wash the slime off as it may contain poisons.

WHEN EATING KILLS

Never eat wild berries and mushrooms. An amazing 95% of white and yellow berries have poison in them. Many wild mushrooms can kill too.

Deer are tasty but difficult to catch. Like all mammals, they must be skinned and gutted before eating.

There are no poisonous freshwater fish, although all fish should be cooked before eating.

SURVIVAL FACTS - DID YOU KNOW?

The moonseed plant is found in woods and has blue/purple fruit that looks like wild grapes. But it is very poisonous and can cause seizures and even death.

Dig for frogs in the mud at the bottom of a pond. If you can, cook frogs before eating.

TRUE STORIES
The U.S. has 10,000 cases of poisoning due to eating wild mushrooms every year. It mostly happens from July to September. Two-thirds of the cases are children.

Insects are easy to find and nutritious Avoid those that are hairy or brightly coloured.

Drop a worm into clean water. It will clean itself, and can then be eaten raw.

Signal for Help

Rescue teams may use planes or helicopters, so marking out an "SOS" signal on clear ground is a good idea. "X" means medical aid is needed. Letters can be drawn in the dirt or snow with a stick, or by scraping with the feet. Make them as big as you can. If possible the letters should be a different colour from the background.

CATCHING THE EYE

Plastic bags and bandannas, in bright colours, can be pegged out on the ground to catch the eye of rescuers above. Anything shiny can be used for signalling in an emergency. People have used CDs, aluminium foil and even the hologram from a credit card.

BEING HEARD

Most survivors are found by searchers on the ground. That's why a whistle is vital on any trip into the wild. Signal for help with six loud blasts on the whistle, a one minute silence, then six more blasts. Three whistles back means help is on the way.

Mobiles can be invaluable but don't rely on being able to get a signal.

SURVIVAL FACTS - DID YOU KNOW?

A search and rescue team will discover as much as they can about the skills, health and personality of the lost person. That way, they have a better idea of where to look.

A whistle can be heard over 1 km away. Your voice carries only a few hundred metres.

TRUE STORIES

Alaska 2004. A dog called Brick was lost in a shipwreck. The brave Labrador was found on a frozen island one month later. He used the only help signal he knew... barking!

Smoke flares do not last long, so be sure that rescuers are looking for you before using.

Spread out flat, a bright bandanna catches the eye. It has numerous other uses, including a sling.

Signal mirrors are small, but on sunny days, the flash can be seen up to 25 km away.

All in the Mind

I will never give up. I will survive. That's the way to think when lost in wild. Survival skills help people stay alive for days, weeks, even months, but only if they fight every inch of the way. Those who give up hope are more likely to die.

BRAIN POWER

It's hard to keep going when you are cold, wet, hungry, thirsty, tired, and perhaps injured. The most important thing is not to panic. Plan what you will need to do survive and think about how you can signal your position to your rescuers.

MENTAL BOOST

Learning survival skills in the wild can help people when they go back to the real world. Knowing they can cope when the going gets tough gives them a lift. Even if they never need their survival skills, knowing they are there makes them feel good inside.

With the right knowledge and skills, a person can survive almost anywhere on earth.

Nature doesn't care about academic ability. It's practical knowhow that will keep you alive.

SURVIVAL FACTS – DID YOU KNOW?

If you hear strange noises in the night in the wild, yell at the top of your voice. The noise will scare away wild animals and lead rescuers to you.

A bivvy bag is waterproof and windproof and keeps in warmth.

TRUE STORIES

Utah, 2005. When children are lost, they usually walk downhill. But 11-year-old Brennan Hawkins walked uphill, over a mountain ridge. It took rescuers four days to find him.

Tarpaulins can help build a shelter or collect water.

A Swiss army knife contains many tools that are useful in a survival situation.

Types of Wilderness

There are many areas of wilderness left in the world. These are places where you will rarely see another person. Living in the wilderness requires skill – but even some basic knowledge will improve your chances of surviving.

Rainforest

Tundra

Forest

Grassland

Desert

Mountains

Glossary

Antiseptic wipes
Small pieces of cloth that contain a chemical which is able to destroy bacteria.

Avalanche
A sudden and unexpected fall of snow down a mountainside, that also contains rocks and ice particles and may sweep away anything in its path.

Bivvy bag
A waterproof drawstring bag, useful as a shelter in an emergency.

Canyon
A deep gorge or ravine in mountainous territory.

Compass
An instrument with a dial and a magnetized needle that points North, and can be used to find directions.

Condense
Return to its liquid state. Condensation is seen when particles of moisture in warmer air come into contact with a container that is cooler.

Exposure
Without shelter from extreme weather conditions, including heat, cold, wind, rain or snow.

First aid kit
A small bag or box containing emergency medical supplies such as bandages, adhesive plasters and antiseptic cream.

Flint
A piece of hard mineral (a type of quartz) that produces sparks when it is struck against steel and can be used to start a fire.

Frostbite
Swelling caused by exposing parts of the body to extreme cold, which sometimes leads to gangrene and amputation of the affected finger, toe or even a limb.

GPS (Global Positioning System)
An electronic device that sends out signals so its position can be tracked accurately anywhere in the world.

Heatstroke
Exhaustion or a range of reactions such as shivering, headache or vomiting, caused by exposure of the body to extreme heat.

Hypothermia
Lowering of the body temperature caused by exposure to extreme cold, which can lead to death.

Iodine tablets
Tablets that contain the chemical iodine, which can kill bacteria in dirty water and make it safe to drink.

Map
A plan of an area printed on paper or plastic, which marks out recognizable features of the landscape.

Snow cave
A shelter made by digging a hollow in snow.

SOS (Save Our Souls)
A call for help, made either electronically or by using something like a flag or smoke signal.

Sun cream
Cream which is applied to parts of the body that are exposed to the sun to protect against sunburn. The higher the factor number on the container, the more protection it gives.

Swiss army knife
A knife with many different useful attachments, first developed for members of the Swiss army.

Tarpaulin
A waterproof sheet that can be folded and carried in a rucksack.

Wilderness
An area that is not cultivated or inhabited.

Index